You Deserved A Lullaby Too

A reflection on healing pregnancy and infant loss

killy alejandro

You Deserved A Lullaby Too

Copyright © 2024 by Killy Alejandro

Williams&Sanders Publishing Company.

Williams0SandersPublishingCo@gmail.com

First paperback edition November 2024

ISBN 979-8-218-53892-7 (Paperback)

Editor: Shawn Alejandro.

Illustrated by: Rein G.

Dedicated to River,
My little girl.

Contents

Preface

Now that this book is in your hands, my daughter gets to exist outside the confines of my mind and heart.

She gets to be somewhere other than a small purple urn under lilies beside a rocking chair. Thank you for helping my baby girl into the world, and though she isn't breathing, please know that means everything to me.

This most devastating loss will grow flowers upon its grave, hopefully flowers to help you grieve with me. I started writing every time my daughter crossed my mind, after she passed away in my belly.

I had no idea what wildfire of emotions awaited me beyond the gates that were closed in my heart.

Of all the poetry I've written and never published, I'm proud to say my first collection is in her name. Published a little before the date she would have been born. My family thanks you, whoever it is that is reading the words that came from our loss.

Your time and attention to the poetry you are about to read means more than any condolences a person could give. To any parents reading that are coping with loss, I see you, and you are the reason these thoughts are being said out loud. The isolating loss of our children can be a little lighter today, as we share in the grief.

From the bottom of my heart, thank you for deciding to pick up this book. Allowing me catharsis in knowing, someone else knows River existed, and was loved. This book is a prayer for our children. A response to the soft sobs from a rocking chair. Your grief is known. Welcome to the community of very few.

The Rising Of A Wave

The blanket beside the empty crib

My love, I know it must be hard,
Sitting alone in a recliner meant for two.

I know it must be weary,
To stare at a nightlight, not meant to protect you.
Your face turned away,
The teddy bear playing night guard from the cradle.

Bottles on the feeding stand,
Right beside the warmer.
Blankets folded neatly on the shelf,
Never to be worn.

My love I know it is hard,
To be a mommy without
a baby.

To be a port in the storm with no ship to come,
A lighthouse standing alone, guiding no one at all.

I see it in your eyes,
I know you see it in mine,
Grieving,
Loving them from afar.

Lingering in the nursery,
Holding on to photos in black and white,
The sounds of the beating hearts we grew.
Desperate to remember the sounds.

My love please remember,
This loss that consumes you,

Only exists to help remind you,
Of all the love that consumed you too.

Sacred Prophecy

I had a dreams of a baby born at home alone,
Before the world stopped spinning.

I would have her alone.
She would wail to the heavens announcing herself,
I would sigh and cradle her small head.
I dreamt of it every night,
between the waking for nausea

And she would be beautiful,
She would look like my son. Big brother,
A grin that rose all the way to my eyes

My family will be complete,
I thought every moment of it,
how full my heart was becoming
The perfect little two and that was all.

Her birthday and his closer than a week apart,
Only two years between them
I thought of it constantly,
Between sips of tea and toddler bedtimes

Oh how beautiful it would have been,
If she were not born in a bathtub when I was all alone.
Six months too soon.

She did not wail,
She did not breathe.
She looked a little like my son,
A little like an angel.

A prophecy to be fulfilled,
My daughter was born at home, in a bathtub.
Born only to death and not to me
The departure settling in,
Stuck between my lips like taffy.

Nothing could have prepared me,
It was a lightning strike in broad daylight with no rain.
A wave crashing as soon as it had risen.
The dawn breaking over midnight skies.

It made no sense at all.
My arms stretched out to no one,
For I was alone.
Reaching for god, until I could reach no further.

I was only a mother,
Calling for anyone to save me
For anyone to hold me.

But all was quiet,
He did not answer my screams.
For he was caring for a baby
And I was grieving
for my daughter.

The numbers game

The long walks in September.
The cooling portal from summer to winter.
This was supposed to be filled with baby kicks.
Something playful and light.

Strangers grinning at your belly asking when your due
And instead they stop and ask,

Is this your first?

Looking at my boy, who two came before,
Two that never took a breath

And one who came after,
The one who just nearly missed the window
Into the world.

Four, I wanted to say.

One, I have one living son, I said.

And their faces turn sour watching you say it,
As if they are almost sorry they asked.

I'm so sorry, I didn't know...
How old were they when they died?

They were never born, I miscarried.

And your heart wells to the brim with longing.

That doesn't count.
You don't need to talk about them like they died
I felt the little twitches and movements.
I picked names,
Watched them wiggle on a screen,

It happens all the time you'll get over it.

I never did,
How could I ever heal,
The wound left by the death of my children.

What a smooth conversation
A monday walk over autumn leaves
Crunching beneath my boots
Swirling around the wheels of a wagon

A wagon meant for two.
Occupying only one.

Psalm 139-13

When I reach for answers in the dark,
My fingers stumble.
Clumsily knocking into the old stories.
The things women told me,
When I was nothing but a baby.

Gatherings of blue water and warmth.
The mist of mornings long ago.

I find the voice of God,
Somewhere in the back of my memories

Can you hear me?
Are you listening?

The air is different,
It tastes like childhood.
It tastes like life before.

God did you plan for my body to be a grave?

Have faith.

I convince myself.
I see no walking on water,
I see no lifting of ash and bone from my eyes.

Have faith.

A candle lit in an empty room
Right in its center,
And there I am,
Searching for a light switch.
Gazing into the black windows,
Searching for a reason why.

Have faith.

Mary felt this way once,
Her boy was stolen from her arms. God how
lonesome this is,

To be stolen from.

Have faith.

But I do not hear,
I cannot hear it yet.

I'm too consumed,
Searching for faith
In the corners of the room.

The stars and the sea

If I am lucky enough
If I am right in thinking that there is a heaven,
There is a chance,
Someday all of my children will be with me.
I will be surrounded with it,
The little voices I never got to know in life.

The mystery of it all,
The grief will never be cured.
Surrounded by the angels,
The ones that gave me motherhood,
Oh a day that will be.

When we are heaven and earth.

And if there is nothing,
The oh, so perfect stillness
The circle of the universe,
Growing, begging to be anything but small.

In the end we all are together once again,
Flowing from one place to another

The synergy of our souls,
Finally in the perfect alignment we missed on earth.

Perhaps my babies are stars
And I will become the sea,

So I may hold them,
Rock them in my waves every night,
Oh a day that will be.

When we are stars and the sea.

All my love

For a moment only,
I was the only soul in the entire universe,
That knew you existed.
I became someone new,
Someone who would give anything to meet you.
For only a few minutes, it was you and I.
All I could feel was hope.
The hope you would live long enough for us to say,

'hello.'

Three slow, tired months I carried you,
Through the ending of a beautiful summer.
The moon beaming onto my shoulders
And the sun found me in its glory.
For every moment of that symbiotic existence,
We were one, one in the same.

In the final moments I knew you were gone.
I knew somewhere that you had left me,
A mother always knows, somehow.

I ached to prove how much I wanted you,
That if only they re-read the scans,
they would find you sleeping.

The lack of movement from your small arms,
Was simply exhaustion from how much
you were alive and growing.

But we would never say hello.
The home I returned to would never be the same.
All my love lost within the deadspace.
Suddenly there was silence.
No more imagining calling your name,
And watching your chubby feet run down the halls.

Instead I found myself staring through tears.
Staring at the tiny body that I failed to make whole.
I loved you,
I love you.

I'll carry you again, just in a different way.
The ashes set beside lilies and roses,
A candle that smells of pumpkin and coffee.
I will love you enough for the both of us,
For the rest of my life.

Hello my love,
I say it in prayer,
And I say it with all my love.

The meaning of words.

The doctor looked cold when she said it,

Pregnancy tissue.

No longer were you my little love, or my baby.

Medical waste.

The flickers of your heart,
The sweet sway of your littleness,
It captivated me the moment I saw you.

Leftover material.

You were always my baby,

The ultrasound showed Fetal demise.
My baby died, why do they say it like that?

No cardiac activity.
Her heart stopped, and no one was crying except me.

No fetal abnormalities.

My little girl was healthy, and now she is gone.
And no one stopped for a moment to call her baby.

You were always my baby.

Prayer for warmth, a prayer for peace

Silver dust spills into the room, and moonbeams
sparkle as I look fondly over the trees.

Fireflies flit over the closed morning glories,
her birth flower.

This night is filled with radiance, the quiet sort
that only holds space in the summer evenings.

It feels impossible to move myself and look away,

But I do,

And I carry you to bed with me, my baby.

The prayer of nighttime washes over me,
pillows that smell of Lily and cotton.

I don't pray on my knees, *I pray with my head down.*

I beg my mother to intercede,
I beg her to guide my words to her son.

I ask for peace… *I trust you.*

I beg for mercy…
I ask for her back, and I hear nothing.

I beg for her safety and I feel desertion.

Oh how my faith has abandoned me.

I think of Mary,

Oh the curse of being a mother to a child and to death.

The coolness washing over me,
a break from the heat of heartache.

The mercy of grief.

I gaze once more at my baby in my room,
covered in a thin handkerchief….
I hope her urn isn't cold.

My baby, my daughter.

My River

Hospital lullaby

I remember the first time I heard it,
The slow twinkling lullaby.
It played from the ceilings in the hospital,
It played through the floors too.
Every week going back I would hear it.

The background noise to my ultrasound,
the echoes of another family with a living baby.
Such a beautiful sound, a war cry of accomplishment.
A mother lingering in the space between
being a portal and a human being.

Every ultrasound I would hear it,
Another child, to another family.
One day it would be my turn.

And suddenly there I was, on a beautiful morning,
the last day of March.
The windows thick with humidity and the dawn.

Pushing the button that played his first lullaby.
Finally, a living baby,
a baby I could take home with me.

He was so beautiful,
I fought tooth and nail to keep him alive.

And I loved that sound ever since, the beautiful
little siren announcing the entrance of a soul
from its mother.

Until I heard it from the emergency room
On a mournful September morning.
I knew before they said it.
The mournful look upon the radiologists face,
It gave her away, the eyes never lie.

The music played, another living baby to another family.
And there I was, once again, losing a piece of me.
Never to return, something time will never heal.
How can you save someone that lives inside you?

The background music, for the news that she had been
dead for weeks, her mother none the wiser.
I will remember that feeling for the rest of my life.
The pain of knowing, she will never hear her first lullaby.

The windows would never be laden
with the humidity of her birth.
There would be no first birthday in a hospital room.
No one would even notice she was missing
Except for me, I would always know.

A moment in time lost to the fabric of reality.

I will never stop wishing for that moment.
Where I would see her eyes flutter open
To the sound of the little song in the hospital.

A girl lost in time, to the fabric of reality.

#193

I pictured the two names side by side on papers,
The pictures lining our home of you and your brother.

How would I pin down a good name?
Something you would love,
I wanted you to think it was beautiful.

Names came and went without much notice,
You were a girl.
I wanted to give you a name
that you could wear with pride.

I always wanted a daughter.

I hope you would have loved your name.
I hope that it was whispered in your ear
when you left me.
Hearing my prayers for you each night,

When I picture you in my minds eye,
Deep in the dead of night, I see you.
The visions of who you could have been.

How am I supposed to miss a baby
that I never got to keep?
How do you grieve a smell from someone's head
Or the softness of someone's skin?

How do I put the pieces of you together
that I never had?
How am I supposed to keep a memory alive
With one one to remember with me?

This is how it feels,
This is how it must feel,
To mourn the death of yourself too.

The Crashing Of It Too

A community of very few

There is a solace in knowing,
I am not the only one. It's a lonely thing,
To be the vessel of life and death.

I'm sorry for your loss.

And they are,
And they love you,
But somehow it seems maybe you were the only one.
The only one who loved the person that died.

A funeral for one,
Grieving first steps and a smile of a mouth
with no teeth.
Grieving the first time you hear them speak.
Grieving a graduation.
Grieving the person you were before.

Its like missing the warmth of a fire that never was lit,
Or the smell of a place you've never been.
Craving a touch that you've only ever imagined,
Or hearing a song that was written but never sung.

At least it was early.

I would do anything for one more day,
For one more day of feeling the life inside of me.
All that remains are the scars she left.
The innocence of knowing that life
will exist through you,

And the sorrow of it being torn from your fingers
still locked tight together, desperately holding on.

There is solace in knowing I am not alone,
That there is another mother beside her sleeping child,
Attempting to cease the visions,
Of two babies on a swing set.
That there is a man comforting his wife,

Unable grasp that she has now become
a new human being.
A woman who has known death,
now from the inside out.
Experiencing the thickness of that departure,
Small bodies relying on you to let go.

Both casket and caregiver.
And It's no one's fault.

They simply existed and then left.
The world never stopped turning.
The sun kept rising.
The fires kept burning.
Our hearts kept beating.

Passing the due date alone.
Wondering what could have been.
Packing the baby supplies away,
Running fingertips over knit yarns
with no one to warm.

Because the world kept going,
Leaving you behind.
Watching everyone else live their lives,
Unknowing of the tragedy.
It's a jealous thing,
Pleading for one more moment of existing with them.

Attempting to pull yourself from the edge,
Only to find grace there.
Right in the thick woods of loss,
There is an allowance in that place.
The community of very few,

And yet so many.
Allowing you to find solace
In a conversation where no one speaks a word.
It's an ugly thing, losing a child.

Chained to the memory,
Of life *before* the world left you behind.
Of a life unborn and lost to time.
They seem to understand...

This community,
Of very few.

Stardust Memorial, Wiseman mortuary

The funeral march,
My son and husband waited behind,
As I walked our baby girl inside.

Here to pick up?

Dropping off, I said.

Her eyes fell to my hands,
Cradling a box swathed in a knit
purple and white blanket.

It felt silly,
To have a belly *without* a baby
 but to still clutch it and cry.
I used to hold my son,
When he was the size of an orange and smaller,
while I cried.

Mommy's ok... I would say to him.

The lady in black took me to the crematorium,
Guiding me with both hands to the building
across the road.

Sign here: Mother,
Release of remains.
Date of birth: September first.
Date of death: September first.
Name: River Alejandro.

The Crematorium manager held me as I began to weep.
The last time my little girl would be whole,
The last time I can hold her outside of an aluminum vase.

The sound I made,
The cry I had only heard about in movies and books.
Unfathomable tragedy, an unending longing,
The sound of a person walking over coals slowly.

She promised me, before I gave her over.

I will be so gentle,
I will care for her as if she were my own....

And she did, she held her with care.
She called her *baby*.
And she called me *momma*.

For the first time I felt like someone knew
what was happening.

Someone finally said it out loud,
She was here, and someone could say it to me
I was momma and she was baby.

We weren't medical waste and patient.
We weren't tissue and 21 year old female.
We were just as we were supposed to be.

And we never would be again.

Tuesday Lilies

There is now a place in my home
where all the pieces of you remain.
Right beside the recliner that should have rocked you.
A vase of rotating flowers.

Some weeks lilies and others pink roses.
Just under a windowsill,
those beautiful cottage windows.
The ones you should have grown up looking through.

You rest there in a perfect little nook.
A handkerchief as a blanket,
A Saint Jude pendant beside you.

Though you stay there alone,
On a little shelf built just for you.
You are never alone.

There is no fear,
The worst has come and gone,

And now you may rest under Tuesday lilies.
Mommy is always close, watching over you.

Too beautiful

There has to be a reason.
Perhaps God knew she would suffer greatly,
And perhaps she was too beautiful
for this spoiled world.

To be human is to suffer beautifully,
I wish I got to mother her through humanity.
Instead of losing myself within the pages in books
about moving on.
My eyes wander over the stages of grief
backwards and upside down.

There must be a reason,
That she never got to feel the sun on her face.
That she never got to feel fuzzy socks in a bed
of clean sheets.

There must be a reason that I will never hold
her hand and walk across a road.
There must be a rhyme to the tragedy.
She will never hear an ocean wave crashing
upon the shore,
Or the sand beneath her feet.

The day before I lost her,
I dreamt I held her by the ocean.
It was dark, and it was cool.
The salted air kissed her dreamy features.

There must be a reason,
And yet there isn't.

Only the dreams of her soul,
The image of what her face would have been.
The ghost of my girl.

Washed away by a wave in a dream.

The universe in a person.

A warm home,
Candles lit in clean spaces.
Throw blankets around the room,
For wherever one may need to hide.

Groceries and flowers from my mother on the counter.

Condolences.

They are grieving the idea of a baby.
And I am grieving a universe.

The candles smell of Chai tea and clean laundry.
The scents don't conflict,
They live above and below each other.

I haven't left the recliner in days,
But my home is warm.
It is clean,
And there are places to hide.

What more could I ask for?

Maybe if I could just have the universe back.

Perfect little worlds

My son, he was dancing before the sun fully rose.
Twirling around the room,
Dressed in freshly cleaned fluffy yellow pajamas.

He is so effortlessly happy,
I watch him and pray for him to always feel this way.

To hear of his sister someday
And not feel the weight of it all.
Beyond his perfect little world, is my own.

He lives within it and around it,
Without seeing the ruins.
My little boy made me smile that day,
Despite all the blood.

In spite of the countless showers,
Washing death off of my legs.
My little boy made me grin from ear to ear today.

I prayed for *this,*

God has not forgotten me.

Cinnamon Roll Coffee

Espresso and fresh October air,
Windows down, heater blowing softly.

My son is rubbing sleep from his eyes in the backseat.
Soft and slow music ripples in the air,
Flowing out the window,
Leaving its lyrics on the road.

With each beat of my heart I am lighter.
Twenty-five miles per hour,
A sunday when no one is awake.

The first coffee in months.
My baby didn't like coffee,
She would make me throw it up.

Cinnamon and milk,
September has finally ended
its looming thirty days.

The saddening sight of the bathtub.
The heartache of the reclining chair.

To be in the car, where nothing has happened.
To be in a moment unburdened
and sobered by morning.

This moment will never leave me.

Traces

A sweatshirt in the color heather gray,
Two sizes too big,
It would have been perfect.

Pajama pants that stretch,
Skincare without retinol,
Peppermint oil and crackers still on the nightstand.

Appointment reminders for ultrasounds,
A baby swing in a box.
The sterilizer under the sink,
The crib in the closet, saved just for you.
Newborn clothes that your big brother wore.

What do I do with the traces of you?

How do you clean out the room of someone
Who has never lived in it?

Humming

I used to sing,
It was this sweet little song in gaelic.

I never knew what it meant,
Only that it soothed my baby sister years before.
I sang it to my son, the day he was born.

The song made sense, the rhythm clicked.
I saw his eyes as I sang it.
He was so small, his eyes had no definite color
hazel, blue, or green?

Definitely blue.

Your eyes would have been brown.
I can feel it in my heart,
It would have undone me at the seams.
Looking into those perfect little glistening eyes.

When I dream of singing to you,
I see your eyes.
Your brother holds your very small hand and we sing.

Oh how cruel it is to wake.

To live in a world where a song aches,

To forever search for eyes I've never seen.

I used to sing, and now all I can bear is to hum

There is no melody now,

Just the silence between.

In the spaces that could have been your heartbeat.

Forever left humming, to the sounds of nothing.

Warm banana bread and cinnamon butter

The coffee drips into the pot below,
This is a *perfect* morning.
My son smiles,
He giggles and plays with the drapes.

The dawn,
The light,
The softness.

Warm banana bread on the plate beside me,
Cinnamon butter dripping off the side.

The recliner that has seen no horror,
My husband is reading beside my son.

And our baby is rocking slowly while she sleeps.
In the swing we bought for her.
We are still whole, and everyone is alright.

She smiles for the first time,
I don't even have time to take a picture.

We go on a walk,
Going to church would be too loud.
The trees smile down at us.

Sun beaming through clouds,
A stroller built for two.

We kiss one another as we walk,
You never treated me any differently.
You never saw me *begging* for God's mercy
While covered in blood.
You never saw me tear myself into pieces.
You never saw a piece of your wife slip away forever.

The walk home filled with laughter,
Our son can hardly contain himself with radiant joy,
It spills from his head to his toes.
He's never seen me broken.

I can taste every moment of the morning on my lips,
From the crisp air to the warm banana bread.

And everything is okay,
I didn't have time to take a picture.

I woke up instead,
reaching for a day that never existed.

Peace be with you

I felt light.
There were no tears left,
Only warms hands.

I found something in this.

It felt light, even in the morning with curtains drawn.
No one was with me,
Only warm hands.

A prayer for peace answered.

For a moment, only one, I was managing.
I could smile at my floor.
Warmth,

This is what I've been waiting for.

The warmth of God.
The peace within,
I knew my daughter was safe.

All she knew was the warmth of her mother,
Until one day there was nothing.
I kept her safe her whole life.

The warmth of a mother,
The warmth of God,
The peace in knowing,

My daughter never knew anything but the warmth.

She was never cold,
She was never lonely,
She was never hungry,
She was never unwell.

One day she was with her mother,
And the next she was with God.

There is a peace in knowing no one harmed her
In the inbetween.

The space between a soul in a body
and a soul released.
I'm the only person she's ever known.

There was no surgery,
No doctors prodding her body.

No pain,
No hate.

Only warm hands.

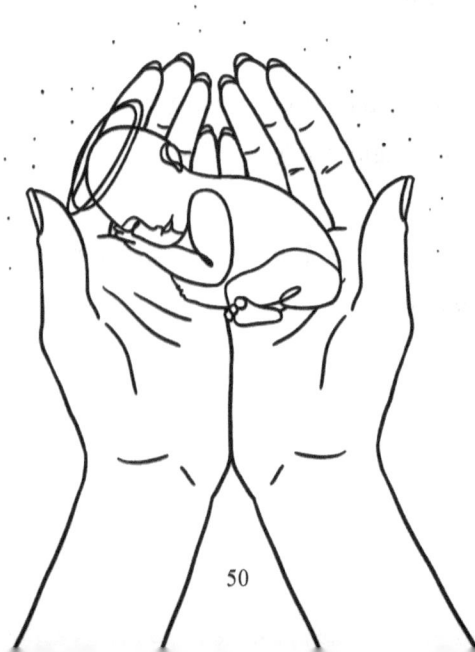

Unconditional

Piece by piece.
It's for you.
Take it all,
Take none if it suits you.

Take my hair,
My hazel eyes,
Take my smile.
My lilting laughter.

Piece by piece.
It's all yours,
Take it all.
Take none if it suits you.

Take my kindness,
My temper too.
Take my expressions,
My funny little freckles.

Piece by piece,
Tear away every piece.
Whenever you'd like,
Whenever you need.

To be a mother is to give yourself away,
Expecting nothing to return.
For you I'll do it willingly,
not knowing if you will ever exist.
All of the energy,
Combining in a moment,
Only to be torn from me again.
Without anything to show for it.
I gave it all away,
Receiving the ashes in return.

The hopelessness of knowing you were of me,
And now you are gone.
Until the second you left,
You were loved,

Unconditionally.

Florida water

Draw the curtains.
Beige against green walls,
Fix the sofa,
Old and thrifted.

Rinse the day away,
Pull yourself together,
Right before you fall apart.
In what dreams may come.

Crawl into a bed,
Soft and dry.
Smelling of florida water,
Lavender essence.

Pray for a moment,
To wake to something beautiful,
To leave it all within sleep,
Maintain the perfect little world.

While missing parts that will never return.

A clock without hands,

It makes time so meaningless.

A car without wheels,

Always headed nowhere at all.

Turkish coffee over fire

The devil couldn't reach me here.
Fire crackling at my feet,
The last fireflies before winter comes.

My husband brewing coffee over the flames,
It was quiet here,
Darkening skies.

The devil couldn't reach me here,
The fires compelling me to speak,
To leave my feelings within its embers.

The tears coming back as steam,
Withering in the cool air.
I saw myself within the flames.

My eyes red and made of glass,
I haven't seen them any other way this month.
The fire was dying,

I saw myself in that too.

Just right

God did not fail me,
I did not fail me.
The doctors did everything just right.

It wasn't an extra daytime nap.
It wasn't the glass of wine before I knew.
Everything was just right.

My husband did not fail me.
My body did not fail me.
Everything was just right.

In the waves of loss,
The ocean of grief,
The riptide that kept me.

Everything was just right,
Until it wasn't,
No one is to blame.

All that's left to do,
Is pick up the pieces.
Trust that one day,
Everything will be just right.

Empty grocery store

Seven.

The grocery store is empty
Do we need milk?
Maybe more rice?
It's so quiet.

Seven-Thirty.

The newborn clothes,
It would have been spring.
The light and airy little girl onesies,
She would have looked so beautiful.

Eight-Thirty.

The maternity section,
I still fit into some of these.
The long sleeved shirts with room to grow,
I would have looked so different.

Nine.

The flowers,
The vase is dead, I should replace it.
All they have are red roses.
My girl needs lilies...

I should really get home,
I've looped the store already.

Ten.

The wine,
Maybe I could have wine.
I'm not pregnant anymore,
I can't take one more reminder.

Eleven.

A shopping cart of milk and lilies,
New maternity pajamas,
The newborn onesie,
We don't need them.

I just can't take one more reminder.

Reaching The Shore

Good morning.

Something feels incomplete.
I forgot to add creamer to my coffee...

No.

There we go.
The peppermint mocha swirled with espresso.

No.

That's better...
It tastes too cold, that must be what's wrong.

No.

My maternity sweater pulled over my shoulders,
It's cold, that's what it is.

No.

My eye catches a blanket I bought for my girl,
There it is...

Yes.

Yes thats whats wrong,
I forgot to put it away with all her other things.

Yes.
I pull the blanket from the recliner and fold it gently,
Tucking it away in a box beneath her urn.

She's so cold.
I cradle the aluminum between my palms.

Yes, that's what's wrong.

Good morning little one…
I'm sorry, I forgot to say hello.

How does one say hello,
When the first greeting ever exchanged was a goodbye?

Like this,
Mournfully.
Full of longing and love,

Good morning.

A muted ocean

The blue sky after the sun has gone,
It settles the nerves in the tips of my fingers.

The tapping stops, the ruminating is over.

The beautiful cottage window stares at me,
Lattice on the panes invite me to stare back.

The sadness ends for a moment...

The perfect shade of deep blue,
A muted ocean captivating the sky above.

A weeping willow peeks at me from the lawn,
It begins to rain.

God has not forgotten me.

All of the weeping I have done,
All that I have lost.

God has not forgotten me.

He has painted the sky, the same shade that would
have become the nursery.
He has given the heavens a reason to mourn with me.

I am not forgotten.
Today heaven mourns with me.

Bleeding pomegranates.
The absence,
Occupies every room in my home,
The absence of your life.
What should have been filled with my tired eyes
And a smile making crows feet.

That special space,
Once filled up with the synergy of a soul.
Leaving me with the ashes of a life in technicolor,
Now in plain black and white.
I knew you alone.

Instead of boiling over,
A pot out of control,
The water is drawing its bubbles back.
I am quiet now.

A whistle from a kettle that never reached heat,
A cup beside a pitcher to never fill,
Tired eyes, and new wrinkles from stress.

Instead of allowing it to envelop me,
I invite it to dinner,
And we speak of you.

In a language only we know.
Over empty glasses and unopened wine,
Empty plates, hearts spilling
over with longing,
Cracked pomegranates
bleeding on the table.

The tea begging to be steeped in water,
What other purpose does it have?
Without the water, we only gaze upon it.

Wondering what it could have been.
But we know what it could have been.
We have smelled that tea before,

We know it would have filled the air
With something perfect,
A hanging scent of bergamot and lavender.

It gives my lip a quiver, the lack of that smell.
I found myself unstitched at the edges.
Over the lack of tea?
No, I am only missing all that should have been.

It informs every step I take,
And every prayer I say.
Quieting my life,
The absence of you.

The wake.

I am a person, existing in the wake.
Existing in the aftermath of a hurricane.

A broken record, skipping through the cycle of loss.
Lighting new candles, sweeping away the fallen petals.

Watching the leaves fall in shades of brown and red.
Proving once again that time is passing.

Watching as women walk by outside
From behind the invisible bars on the door.
And they are as far along as I would have been.

My teeth tearing my mouth apart with mourning
Until I see them smile.

And I smile back.
I cannot sit in the ruins all day,

Ruining the smile of another with my melancholy.

I let the wool wrap against my body
But it does not cover my eyes.

I let it pass,

It's only a walk on an autumn afternoon,
It's no one's fault.
It only feels as if walking past my window,

Is a little like walking past a tomb.

Exodus 14:14

The Lord will fight for you,
You have only to be still.

My body wanted to move desperately,
To go nowhere, to walk endlessly.

I have only to be still.

It was funny, to finally give in.
To allow myself to give my heart up for only a moment.

I have only to be still.

How does the Lord fight for me?
There is no battle to be won.

Only loss to heal.

I have only to be still.

How can I have faith in the stillness?
I see no ghost or apparition,

There is no healing in stagnation.

I have only to be still.

And then I heard it.
The hum of blood in my heart.
The steadiness of my breath.
My bereavement diluted by silence.

There I was, finding faith without looking.

I have only to be still.

The rottenness of loss dripping from my eyes,
It was medicinal,
The cleansing of a room unopened in weeks.

The ending of a storm,
The rage of the wave heading for shore.

I had only to be still.
And so I was.

Toddler toys

I feel it most in the space between notes in a song
The lulling of a scene,
The moments where time stands still.

The view between a mountain and its rivers
The beauty in sorrow.
All of life's imperfections singing together.

I feel it most in the places where no one would expect.
Ordering a coffee, something flavored cinnamon,
I feel the loss within the ordinary.

Buying toddler toys, My son laughing,
Flashing his teeth at me from the cart.

Tears biting at my eyelashes while passing pacifiers.

And it was okay.
The ordinary grief,
The heartbreak known by others.

The pause,
To allow it to exist.

The exhale,
Allowing it to pass.

Rivers and Rocks

I love rivers…
Water playing with the rocks,
Splashing in the currents of their own design.

I love the world beside the rivers,
Slow and still.
Mountains guardian each of its doorways.

I can linger as long as I need.

Cold and welcoming,
Pour the soul into a river,
All of the bruises and scars melt away.

The wounds within that water, \
Baptizing the pain.

I can stay here as long as I need.

Catharsis.

I named my daughter River,
To let her go.

She's in a restful place,
Baptized in the river of her namesake.

Warm Taffy

For years it will linger,
As stone in your pocket.
Or Stars clinging to the sky,
As Flowers rooted within the earth.

The ache, it will linger on your tongue,
It will lace the sentences with hard earned knowing.

People will see it in your hands,
When you hold them close, interlacing your fingers.

They will see it in your eyes,
When every inch of the sky is reflected by your iris.

Living in the world after,
It will reside on your shoulders
And on your face.

All that beautiful love with nowhere to go,
Pressed into your skin like a flower in a diary.

It will linger *forever,*

The deep knowing eyes,
The loving warm hands.
The strong shoulders,
The melancholy face.

It will cling to you like warm taffy,
The signs of someone who truly loved.

Waving hello.

From the shore, under night's wing,
To the sand brightened by dawn,
This is what it feels like.
Watching the ocean dance upon the earth,
No one is with me here.

It is only the water and I.
This is what it feels like,
Allowing blood to pulse within you,
Without eating your heart as it beats.

Warmth of the sun, and the shadows it casts.

This is what it feels like,
To watch life in reverse.
The sea understands,
All of its souls vibrate reaching for your hands.
The ocean knows loss.

It is no fault of the tide,
People lose themselves within it.
In the gravity of the waves,
It is no fault of the moon for her effects.

The sun and the shore wait for you
to let the words fall into the water.
They have nowhere to be,
You can say it here.
You can say it out loud.
Weights lifted off the soul, in a way that *matters*.
No one to punish you for allowing the words to form.
There was never a timeline for this.
There was no registry for *losing* you.

And your eyes will burn,
Your lips will tremble and lose composure.
You will feel the sand begin to sink beneath you,
And the waves to reach closer.

I miss my baby, but I will be okay.

And there it was,
My mouth which had only begged,
My lips which had only cursed.
My teeth had only torn.
They accepted.

The funeral of a mother and her daughter.
Never to be kissed be the sun,
Never to be *known*.
The terms of humanity falling at odds
with being human.

The rising of a wave,
And the crashing of it too,
Watching as it reaches the shore.

This is what it feel like,
To grieve love,
To be in the thickest of loss.
To allow the ache to assist your feet to move,
And forgive yourself for it too.

Gathering love.

The crib in the closet, pulled out and cleaned.
A bassinet covered in dust,
A few cradle sheets.
I stacked everything together neatly.

It was time.

I made sure
they looked beautiful
before I passed them along.

Another baby, to another family.
A woman and her lover,
Grinning ear to ear.

Her husband loading all the wooden pieces into their car,
I watched as they glowed, the sun favoring the spot in
the room where they stood.

Thank you, she said.

There was a sweetness to it, a cruel sort of sweetness.
The memory of my son in the crib that should have
become his sister's.

It will no longer collect dust,
In a pile of things that cannot be used.

The crib will be tended by another set of tired hands,
A sleeping baby that isn't mine,
A morning stretch and smile that I won't ever see
A happy baby that heard the little hospital song,
A baby that survived all the odds.

There was no anger,
No jealousy.
Only love,
Gathering together in the center of my chest.

I watched them leave,
Taking all that remained of my son's babyhood.
The gray cradle, two little teeth marks on the rim.

The bassinet that held my world,
Sheets of muslin and cotton.

The car rolled past the old maples in the yard,
Leaves dancing in the wake of the tires.

I hope it brings them peace,
I hope they love that baby to pieces.

God knows it's a gift,
To be able to love someone who can breathe.
It's a lovely gift, to have tired hands tending to a crib.

I hope the sun favors the spot in the room
where the crib will exist.
I hope there is enough love to drown out all the noise.
It's a gift, having a place for all the emotion,
All that hope spills over, having a place to go.
Erupting like a volcano.

Communion.

There is a friend that comes over nightly now,
We have tea while the day fades away.

Our cups fill, only a little under where they should.
We come into communion with one another,
Having little tea waffles.
And they never quite get warm enough.

Something is missing and she knows it.
We smile at one another.
The long sort of smile,
Thankful for the time we have together.

Our embraces last longer than most others,
It is a comfort that I am afforded.
I live with her now.

She has a drawer in my bedroom,
And a cup in the cupboard.
She comes when the heartache rings in my ears,
Sitting on the couch beside me.

She holds me,
While I bleed from my mouth,
All of the lovely things I needed to say.
She listens, and then she goes.
She will come back, I count on it.

She drapes the dark corners with curtains
made of velvet.
The way she weaves,
It has made this place so warm.

She holds my hands that want to hit,
And legs that kick.
She dresses herself in lines of prose,
When she wraps me in the perfect mourning embrace.
I brush the empty sayings off her shoulders.

I fold her an extra blanket before I go to sleep,
Goodnight, I say to her,

Grief lives with me now, my friend and comfort.
The evidence that love lived with me too.
The reminder of life that once existed.
Goodnight, she says back to me.

Falling asleep reminds me,
As I blink in and out of the world,
Of all the times my mother would sing to me.
Of all the times she would pull a blanket all the way to
My chin and kiss my head, singing a lullaby.

The love I have for my mother,
I hope my daughter would have loved me that much.
That she also might have thought of me
In her hours of loss, as a comfort.

I will have to do with my mother over the phone,
As we age in synchrony.
It is hard to watch us get old together,
But a gift all the same,
To love someone
And watch them grow older with you.

Until I can see my girl again,
In what dreams may come.
Out of synchrony,
Until we are ashes to ashes,
Until we are dust to dust.

I will hum for her, like my mother did for me.
My little River,

She deserved a lullaby too...

Contributors

I want to take a moment to especially thank those that aided in the motivation and creation of this collection. Firstly to my husband, without you, I never would have started writing again. Thank you, my love, for all the support you have given me through our marriage and through our third loss. You have carried me through this ocean of grief like a lighthouse guiding me home.

The next people I need to thank are my close friends and family, for helping me pay for the beautiful artwork and delicate cover design. My beta readers and biggest supporters through my writing. The friendship you have shared with me is truly beautiful beyond compare.

Without you I'm not sure any of this would have made it off my computer.

A special thank you to Stevie as well, for giving me a safe space to display my collection. No matter what, through tough times I knew I could come to you.

There is no shortage of the words I could say to thank the people that have made this possible.

I hope someday, this poet will find the right words to say Thank you.

All my love,

Killy Alejandro.

A letter to the reader:

If you have made it this far, if you have stuck with me through the dragging lines and cycles of loss, thank you. I hope that you found something within the mournings and dreary writings in front of you. That you also may find hope and peace within this feeling.

It's not an easy road to drive, nor the easiest line to walk. I hope within the confines of these pages and this cover you found a place to allow the emotions to flow.

From my heart to yours,
Peace be with you.

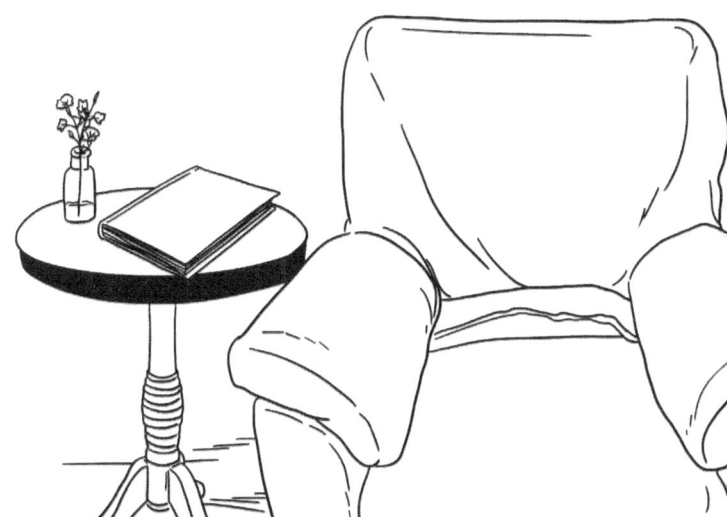

About the Author

Killy Alejandro, a long-time writer, finally emerged into the published world. This collection is the first ever publication of the author. A full time mother and psychology student. The California born writer writes primarily poetry, but also works with other genres to be released soon. This deep reflection and meditation on grief and parenthood came about after the loss of the author's daughter.

To contact the author you can visit
the social media links below.

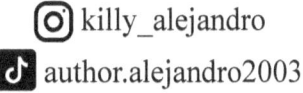 killy_alejandro
author.alejandro2003